The Messenger

Puzzle Piece Publications

A Collection of Poems, Artwork and Photographs
by
Lisa A. Edelbrock

ISBN 0-9720484-5-6
The cover art and all text and photos in this book are the exclusive property
of the author. No part of this book may be used or reproduced in any
manner whatsoever without written permission except in the case of brief
quotations embodied in critical articles or book reviews. The author may be
contacted at laedelbrock@yahoo.com

Puzzle Piece Publications
846 26th Avenue North
St. Cloud, MN 56303

Edited by Tracie Kniazkova and Dave Mercurio

Printed in the United States of America by
MK Group, St. Cloud, Minnesota.

A portion of the net proceeds from the sale of this book go towards funding
the Shelby Eisenschenk Spirit Scholarship at Arc Midstate, St. Cloud,
Minnesota. This scholarship will help in the continuing efforts to support
and educate families connected with individuals with developmental
disabilities.

DEDICATION

For you, Shelby,
my messenger of great faith,
hope and extraordinary love.

To my dearest Sasha,
for being who you are.
You brighten my world.

For my parents,
who I look to for strength;
thank you for all your support.
For you, Dad,
thank you for your special friendship with Shelby.
And especially, thank you Mom,
for showing me the power of a mother's love.

To my friends
who encouraged me to compile my poems
for this book, and fulfill my dream.

For the children.
Who everyday face a
different world from the rest of us.
Who show us their courage,
love, and pure determination.

Contents

FOREWORD

These poems were inspired on the roads less traveled. When reading them, I hope you realize that you are never alone. Someone has been on the journey before you, and there will be others after you.

May you find comfort in the words, maybe a shoulder to cry on, and maybe a reason to let your tears flow. May you understand that these feelings of despair, worry, and loss are all very natural. I hope you will also find all the smiles, laughter, and enjoyment that your soul is yearning for as you journey with a messenger. May you embrace your feelings!

Healing happens only when fear and love, joy and sorrow, smiles and tears can exist within us in a lasting place of peace. The healing happens along the journey; mine can be found in these poems. This collection exposes my daily experiences with doubt, happiness, joy and sorrow. I revisit these poems often. They remind me of where my family has been, how much we have grown, and the gift I have been given.

Reflecting on where we have been is essential to understanding our passage through time. For it is the journey, not the destination, that is important. If you would like to chronicle your own feelings about traveling with a messenger who has touched your life, reflection pages have been provided in the back of this book. These poems are an expression of my thoughts, an insight into my life, and my spiritual journey with my messenger. This is not a story of sorrow, this is a journey of great hope and love.

May you realize that you have been deeply blessed!

Lisa Edelbrock

PASSAGE ONE

My Messenger

"You who do not see us, you who do not hear us, you imagine us in the far distance, yet we are so near. We are the messengers who bring closeness to those who are distant. We are messengers who bring light to those who are in darkness. We are the ones who bring the Word to those who are in question."

~Angel in Far Away, So Close~

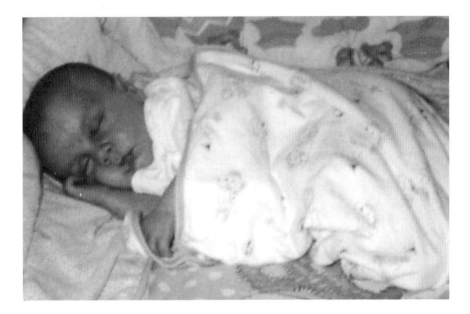

Lisa A. Edelbrock

Your Child

In the darkness,
And the quietness
Of the night

Go peek at your child
And dwell in delight
Of the child that rests.
And with reflection
Touch the outline of the face
That trusts you more
And judges you less.

Trace
The child,
They grow~
So quickly we are told.

Let their gentleness
Pierce your soul.
And you will always know
What it is like to touch the face
And feel the warm embrace
Of love so deeply driven
Of the child you have been given.

My Inspiration

Our family would not be the same
If we did not have
These difficulties in our lives.
We are all who we are,
Because of my son.
It is because of him that I am able to write,
Which in turn helps others express
Their fears and their tears.

He is the messenger,
For without him these
Words and feelings
Would not exist.
They come through him to me,
To the pages you now read.

These are words from the Divine;
Through us, to you.
I may be the person
To live this life of mine.
These words I write come from my hand,
But they are not truly mine.
I am but a vessel,
That God has sent to you.
To help you find your strength,
To give you hope and to help you understand
That although there will be rough times,
The gift of love remains.
These are gifts from the Divine,
Passed from me to you.
To let you know He still cares and to help you
Figure it all out and not get left behind.

Lisa A. Edelbrock

We are all blessed by these souls
And these lessons they have
Been sent to teach.

Embrace the trials and the emotions
They bring.
They are here for a reason.
Let the lessons begin.

Lisa A. Edelbrock

Though angels are both the messengers
and the message of God, that makes them
no easier to receive.
For one thing, we almost never recognize them,
even when they stand before us,
and sometimes hold our hand.

Lisa A. Edelbrock

Epiphany

There was a fog
Deep and dark; the paths were so many,
No way to determine which direction to turn.

So many decisions, so much to do.
A sense of urgency led me on.
To get help, which kind of help?
From whom?
My heart no longer in living,
Just making it through each day.
Depression weighing heavily
On my soul filled with fear.

Then one day in total exhaustion
I sank down and cried.
My soul spilled the tears
Which had welled up inside.
I realized I could not do this alone,
Thinking no one could help us out of our doom.

Your will be done.
A deep trust was formed.
At that moment: An infusion
Of grace from the Divine.
I was opened to allowing the healing forces to enter.
Then I recognized
We were not lost to the world
We were not alone.
There was hope.

Stolen

What are little boys made of?

Puppy dog tails,
Frogs in pockets, baseballs bats,
Climbing trees, first dates.

I want these problems.
I'd give anything to change;
This path we are traveling
Is not what I had planned.

I want my dreams back,
I want my son.
He was stolen away,
When he was so small.

I never got to hear his words,
Or find out who he is.
I want that opportunity;
I want back what we had
When he was so small.

Before he was stolen,
Before he entered this world
Of the quiet, the confused,
And the lost.

I will find him again.
That's my job as his mom.
I will find him again.
And hear his first words.
I will be there for him.
I will find him again.

Lisa A. Edelbrock

But until that day,
I will love him and play with him,
We will smile and laugh.
We're on this journey together,
We are on the right path.

For we have one another,
The love it is true,
Love conquers all!!!

Yes, I am talking to you!!

When The Abnormal Becomes The Norm

It scares me so
When it all becomes routine.

It seems so familiar,
Then I step outside my life;
Visit another family, another town.

I see none of what is normal,
And then it dawns on me:
We aren't the normal family.
Life is difficult in our world.

Then I yearn for an everyday life.
I yearn for health,
I yearn for a quiet day.
A day that I know
I will not see for a very long time.

When it all becomes routine,
When the abnormal becomes the norm.

2001

Lisa A. Edelbrock

One Small Child

Each day I fight the war,
Each day a silent battle,
Each day a little more soul energy
Is expanded.

The unknown enemy
Silently has taken this child
One quiet night at home.
I never heard them come,
And now at once they are gone.

This battle I wage is to get him back again.
The price is high;
In this war only the strong survive.
The lessons learned are many, .
The cost is very high,
The war is fought for one small child.
When will it ever end?
I will never know– the toll it takes is extremely high.

Not to fight, is not a thought.

To the victor goes one small child.

Lisa A. Edelbrock

Riptide

Just as when one goes swimming in unfamiliar ocean waters.
You can be swimming and enjoying yourself and all at once
The ocean takes you under,
And you are caught in the riptide.
You have no control; no matter how hard you swim,
The currents pull you under.

The same holds true for a family when their child
Is diagnosed with any special need. The diagnosis itself
Grabs hold, and your family is pulled under.
Pulled under with the shock, the depression, the agony
And the lost dreams that once kept the family afloat.

Now they helplessly drift with the strong currents;
This whole new life threatens their very existence.

These are unfamiliar waters
The current is strong and fast.
Every so often it lets up just a little;
And that is when you must fight with your very
Will to somehow make it to safer waters, and back to shore.

The events of this riptide will change you forever.
You can never forget the moment you were told of the diagnosis,
Or the feeling that something is terribly wrong.
The hard part is to never give up. Keep afloat somehow,
Try to keep your head above the waters,
And try to keep your eye on the shore.
You can make it out of the riptide;
Just believe and never give up hope.

Lisa A. Edelbrock

Dadda

He had about five words:
Dadda, babba, mamma, no, and go.
Then, one by one, they were lost.
Erased from his vocabulary.
Just like when a word is erased from
The chalk board, gone forever–
But a trace of it lingers on.
I cannot remember hearing some of them
Anymore.
I do remember hearing him say
"Dadda" in the early
Morning hours.
Calling, requesting his daddy to
Come and free him from his
Child-proof, gated room.
"I'll go get him," I say,
In my sleepy voice.
"No, he is asking for me;
I'll go get my Buddy Boy!"

That is the last word I remember,
Vaguely over the years.
I don't remember hearing "Mamma" anymore.

Just the sound of a two-year-old calling for
Dadda from his door.
The early morning light
Releasing shadows from his room.

The innocence in that young voice,
Loud and strong and sure!

How were we to know
It was the last word
We would hear.

Lisa A. Edelbrock

Helpless

The seizures take their toll.
Your body shakes, and twitches,
Your body just can't take it. You sleep.

As I watch, helpless,
I mourn for the child that was.
Where have all the dreams gone?
So easily washed away.
Each day my tears erase
A little more of what should have been.

I wish I could take the pain away,
The confusion within your eyes.
I wish I could explain,
I wish you could understand.
All I can do is hold you close,
Let you know that I am near.
Hold you and be the "strong" one,
Try to protect you, but I am helpless.

Until I retreat to shed my tears
For a mother feels the pain, and swallows,
Acknowledging that this is how it will be.
Instead of baseball games
We are doing EEG's.
Instead of soccer matches
We do hospital stays.

It would be nice for once to get a break,
And be the average eleven-year-old boy.

Maybe in our dreams,
Maybe in your dreams,
But for now we are helpless.

8/7/2001

The Vigil

I see people look,
But quickly glance away.
I wonder what they see.

The outside has weathered much,
But can they see the inside me?
Do I show too much of sorrow?
Do the eyes show all the pain?
Does the appearance show the toll?

I'm afraid for them to look,
To inquire how I've been,
For some insightful person
Will ask that hated question:
"So, really, how have you been?"
And I will need to answer,
Softly with fear and dread.

Can I hide the truth?
For it is me I do not trust.
If I opened up for just one minute
My composure I might just lose.
Then I may be lost forever.

So I will continue
This vigil that I keep.
Everything is going fine,
While glancing at my feet.
"And just how are you,
This beautiful summer day?!"

4/15/2002

Lisa A. Edelbrock

Wandering

How could he tell that he could hear?
This I still don't know.
Let's have him tested one more time.
We sat alone in that small room–
Did he really show that he could hear?

We met then, he and I,
And this wandering little soul.
"Yes Ma'am, he can hear."
That's all he had to say.
Then what is wrong with him?
"This I do not know.
All I know is he can hear,
You'll have to get him tested elsewhere."

I felt so bad for praying that my son now would be deaf.
What a terrible thing for a mother to hope.
At least, then, there would be answers,
A direction for us to go.
Instead we leave more confused
As we continue to wander helpless
In his quiet difficult world.

8/2002

Yesteryear

I miss the days of yesteryear,
Of times when I belonged
Of times when people understood,
Or at least I thought they always would.

Now it seems it's so complex,
And no one takes the time
To see what is really true
Within this heart of mine.

I want so to belong with them,
To feel a part of it all.
But sadly I'm an outcast now
To be welcomed never again.

I hope they never have to make
The choice I made that day:
To help the child who couldn't,
Or the husband who in his sadness wouldn't.

Sometimes I wish they'd have to choose.
Maybe then they'd understand
The ultimate sacrifice I have made,
To find the child hidden
In the silent world he was given.

They think that I'm the cruel one.
Just leaving the way I did.
They think I had another.
Oh, how wrong they all have been.
They think that I stopped loving–
Of course that's what I said.
I had to tell them something,
Or I couldn't have done what I did.

Lisa A. Edelbrock

The father hurt and lost wouldn't or couldn't help the son who needed him.
The time called for desperate measures, and so I took the blame
For hurting their son and brother and breaking the family apart.
The family had been struggling,
Long before they had a clue.
I tried to do my best, but there's only so much one can do.

So now the solitude is mine–
Except for the two souls that I guide.
But I'd love for them to know
I didn't take the easy way out; I took the upper road.
I'm trying to help the children,
I know it may sound strange.
I had to find help for Shelby;
If those around us were not helping,
Then they became my foe.
I had to help this silent child.
So now I spend my hours guiding and teaching,
Caring and supporting.
But what I did was also for them, you see.
The needs of the one outweighed the needs of us all
In those blurry, early chaotic days.

I've learned patience, and understanding,
And giving of oneself.
But most of all it's just because,
It's the thing I felt I had to do.

When given a child with special needs, the special one is you.
The giving never stops, the teaching never ends, and the advocate speaks out.
The virtue is patience; the loving never ends.

The Messenger

So it holds true for the dad
Left behind that day–
Someday maybe they will see.
The choice never truly was mine, on that snowy, wintry day;
We had to follow the path set in front of us
Or be forever left behind in the world that waits for no one,
And cares about those left behind even less.

I will always care for the man I left behind that day.
I had to play the cold one,
To do what I did that day.
I know he'll never forgive me.
I hurt his soul, it's true.
He loved us in his own way, but my heart is broken too.

We both were hurt so deeply, living our separate lives.
It just seemed the only way to help those two children of mine.

I'm sorry for the pain, and the heartache this has caused,
In trying to provide a better environment
For the children, in which to grow and learn.
I had to break up what was once to them a loving family.
Maybe someday all will know the truth.
I'm sure it will be too late.
For now their father won't even talk to me,
And the best word for me is hate.

If only we could have talked
And shared our fears and our tears.
If only he could have entered the world that had
Trapped us both.

Lisa A. Edelbrock

We were both so isolated then,
Not knowing how to approach the subject,
Not knowing what it meant to us all.
If only he could have helped with the programs of this young child,
I wouldn't have done what I did–
If only he could forgive me, and learn from what we've been through.
If we could just talk things through, then perhaps
The solitude may just end.

And so I live with what I did
That early winter morn.
I know we both hurt tremendously.
But I wanted you to understand in some small way
Why I did what I did.

9/23/2000

Lisa A. Edelbrock

Can You Believe

It all came rushing back today when I spoke
With the mother of this young boy.
She had so much sorrow; I could hear
It through the telephone wires.
So many questions– so few answers,
The burden taking its toll.
So much fear for what lies ahead
And not much faith in herself.

It is hard to explain the journey we're on;
It is hard to explain–my faith.
It is hard to explain you must put your faith
In the lad that's been entrusted to you
And believe.

She questioned the saying,
"Does God give you more than you can handle?"
I tried to explain, I didn't think so,
You just have to believe in yourself.
He gave you His child because He knew
You would love him in spite of yourself.

Your courage will grow with your knowledge.
I know it is overwhelming, this is true.
One day at a time is all He asks;
He will bring the right answers to you.
They may not come when they are expected;
The road is a long one, it is true.
They might not be the ones asked for,
But they will bring peace to you.
The peace may not come for a while,
But it will come when you start to believe.

Looking back now I see us where you are.
We were there too,

The pain is still strikingly new.
I remember being lost as you are.
And no, I am not better than you.
I have cried the same tears you now cry
I have asked the same questions, too.
The one difference I can hear right now is
I have asked for help, and it was given.
Given in ways I was unsure.
Given to me in spite of myself,
Given by some who had journeyed before,
Given by some who just knew.
Given by many who believed.

This child you are guiding will change you.
But first you must believe in yourself.
You did not do wrong in his coming.
There is no blame to spread anywhere else.
This child has been sent for a purpose,
Your family selected because you care.
You will learn much from this soul you are guiding.
Just look into those eyes and see.
Trust in this blessing you've been given.
Trust in yourself and believe.

If you say you don't have religion,
Now is a good time to question as any.
To ask the One above for His help and His strength;
The strength that you need to just make it through
The rest of these very long days.
Each day ask for help and for strength;
Each day ask for patience to spare.
Each day see the child,
Each day see the smiles,
See the good in the lad you are leading.
And the rest will take care of itself.

Yes, you will have to be vigilant.
Yes, you will need to confront.

Lisa A. Edelbrock

Yes, you will need to be constant.
And most of all, yes, you'll continue to love.
Yes, you will need to be hopeful,
For hope opens the doors that are locked.

All the higher power is asking of any of us
Is, "Will you look after my angel,
Who cannot yet fly by himself?
Will you help my small angel?
Do you have enough
Faith, hope and love?"

If your answer is yes to the questions,
If you see the spirit looking at you,
Your life you see will be changed for the better
By the eyes of the angel
Standing looking at you.

Looking to you for some help;
Looking to you for some peace.
Looking to you for much love;
Looking to you to believe.

That he is a blessing that was sent,
That you will help him along.
That you will strengthen his spirit
And he will heal yours
With his smiles, his laughs, and his hugs.
So believe in this spirit you are guiding.
Yes, he is special, it is true.
Believe he will change your world
And, yes, it will be for the better.
Because it is built on all that is needed,
Built on the strongest of foundations,
Built on your faith, your hope and your love.

9/30/2002

Lisa A. Edelbrock

Eleven

No longer a toddler,
Not yet a teen,
Growing older and taller.

It's not what was dreamed,
He will no longer catch up.

That hope now is gone.
No longer the dreams,
"It's just what boys do."
No longer the dreams,
"He is only two."

Now he is eleven,
Almost a teen.
He is in his own little world,
And we can't be let in.

I can no longer believe
That he will catch up.
Lost dreams, lost goals
No longer are seen.

New goals are made
To make it through.
New dreams are thought of,
But don't come true.

Hard to get rid of those
Young motherhood dreams,
How silly they seem now;
Oh, how naïve.

2001

　　　　　　　　　　　　　　　　Lisa A. Edelbrock

Discovery

They gather here with hopes
And excitement for another year.
They greet friends with laughs
And hugs and smiles
And energy to spare.

There are those who enter quietly
And do not say a word.
There are those who become
Overwhelmed by the excitement in the air.
This school stuff can be overwhelming–
The noise, the people, the turmoil
Surrounding us everywhere.

I wish I knew how to comfort you,
So you feel you do belong;
I wish you would have some friend to greet,
Instead of the unfortunate stares.
The looks of those that don't understand
And those trying to be polite but
Aren't quite sure.

Soon tears begin to run;
It is all too hard for you.
Perhaps mainstreaming isn't the best.
Perhaps I want to believe.

I want to believe you belong here,
Here with all the rest.
I want to believe you'll make some friends;
I want to believe you will belong.

I want to believe you'll learn so much in school.
Perhaps, child, I am wrong
To watch you on these difficult days,
It shakes my beliefs to the core.
If you don't belong in this place, then
Just where do you belong?

8/28/2002

Lisa A. Edelbrock

Traveler's Spirit

A strong combination of spirit and soul
Lost in a vessel,
With a definite beginning and
A definite end.
Where it will lead?
No traveler knows.

This ship, it is lost.
No compass to guide,
No stars to guide the way,
Looking desperately for a
Safe harbor.

No safety along the way–
Only rocks and swells
And torn sails.
The winds do die.
However, the traveler has lost
All bearing,
No time between the gales.

The boat is steady,
The boat is strong,
But so now is the storm.

The traveler's spirit is
What determines all.

Will he succeed or fail?

2002

Lisa A. Edelbrock

Life Of Numbers

He was in the womb for nine months,
Born at 11:25 in the morning on the
Third day of the eighth month,
In the year nineteen hundred and ninety,
Weighing seven pounds, three ounces,
And nineteen and a half inches long.
He has one big sister.
Had shots at nine months,
Diagnosed at two-and-a-half.
The search to find much help for the child
Does better if reached before the age of five.
Went to school at the age of three,
Rediagnosed by four.
Started kindergarten at age six.

We have been through five speech therapists,
Six OT's, and somewhere on this journey
I lost count of all the personal care attendants.
He has been in three schools, has had five aides.
He will transition to his fourth school,
Will be in the seventh grade.
He will be in school till the age of twenty-two.
He will not drive when he is sixteen,
And probably never marry.

He has touched hundreds if not thousands
Of people along his journey.
He will capture every heart,
Make every one of us smile.
His personality will last a lifetime;
I will cherish him indefinitely and
He will stay within our hearts
For all eternity.

9/2002

In Your Absence

Tonight with your absence
We find a glimmer of what life would be like,
In your absence.

In your absence there is quiet, there is calm,
There is peace.
The whirlwind has calmed,
Our evening is peaceful.
Yet with this calm emptiness
Comes a picture of
How life was meant to be,
Of a family watching a movie together,
The days of yesteryear.
This emptiness has brought back
The longing of what was supposed to be.
Dreams unfinished,
Words unsaid–
Life is not complete.
All these rekindled with just a few
Hours of quiet and a moment of
Your absence.

In this quiet there is also
A longing for that
Giant grin,
Those big green eyes
Looking straight at me.
All these emotions are stirred
In your absence.

Lisa A. Edelbrock

Love Conquers All

"Love Conquers all," the saying goes.
In growing up I wanted to believe that
The fairy tale could come true.
I knew I was strong; I could love someone so deeply
That Love could conquer all.

As I grow older, I now realize
The harsh reality.
Love does not conquer all.
There is no "happily ever after;"
Dreams can crumble down.

My love is strong,
My determination solid and still;
The silence remains,
The disease uncured,
The family broken;
What a harsh reality.
When reality is too much to bear,
Seek within your soul.

The child, he does do well
In his own way– this is true.
Maybe love does conquer all,
For we are not yet at the end:
Maybe dreams can still come true!

3/2002

Master Plan

As I gaze into this sleeping face
I understand my role
Is to guide
This tender, precious little soul.

I now know the role that
God has planned for me.
And I'll do it lovingly.
He cannot tell me thank you
Or help along the way.
Only repays my work with smiles
And short, poignant gazes.
If I do nothing more but this task
In front of me, my life will be complete.

For now I truly understand

The gift in front of me.

Lisa A. Edelbrock

PASSAGE TWO

A Sacred Contract

"Suddenly, almost before he knew it, he was
perched on the lap of the understanding Angel,
and was explaining how very difficult it was for a
boy who suddenly finds himself transformed
into an angel."

~Charles Tazewell,
The Littlest Angel~

You Have To Be Autistic To Understand

What is it like to hear and understand,
To watch others form words with their lips,
So for hours and hours you practice,
But you just can't get
Your mouth to make similar noises to theirs?
After all this trial, you still can't speak any words.
You would have to be autistic to understand.

What is it like to be a small child
In a school, in a room full of sounds?
With children who talk, and talk,
With noises all so very loud?
I try to be calm and understand
But my nerves just can't take it all in.
You would have to be autistic to understand.

What is it like to love the computer?
Because I know exactly what it will do.
The outcomes are always the same,
The routine soothes my soul.
You would have to be autistic to understand.

What is it like to be curious about the world around you?
Searching for knowledge I can call my own.
With an inner desire to understand,
But then it is lost in the confusion within.
At times I need to smell and touch and hold
To figure out my world.
It calms me when I can be myself.
This causes people to look perplexed.
This world is such a unique place.
You would have to be autistic to understand.

Lisa A. Edelbrock

What is it like to enter a room
And all at once you're all confused?
My mind wants to be calm and quiet,
But my body needs to move and bounce.
I know I act differently than everyone else.
But I can't control the way that I feel.
You would have to be autistic to understand.

For parents, teachers and siblings,
I know you get frustrated with me.
Some days I understand what you're saying to me.
Some days I look somewhat confused.
Other days you talk to me and, I swear,
I really don't have a clue.
You would have to be autistic to understand.

What is it like to be stared and sneered at,
Laughed at right in your face?
What is it like to not have a friend?
No one who calls for overnight stays,
Or go to a movie, or to just hang out.
No one saves a seat on the bus,
But they make me look puzzled and confused.
You would have to be autistic to understand.

What is it like to try and speak and try to get
Your message across, when all you see is
Confusion on faces of those surrounding you?
See them not understand the words you try and speak,
Or the finger-talking to try and help them understand?
The frustration sets in because people seldom understand.
You would have to be autistic to understand.

What is it like on the journey of life
To meet with so many strangers
All moving at such a rapid pace?
And you can't understand the look on their faces
Because it is all so different and very new.
And you're lost and all alone.
You would have to be autistic to understand.

What is it like to have to depend
Upon someone who knows you and understands?
Someone who helps with the simplest of things,
Someone who keeps you safe and on course.
Because life is too confusing in this world in which you live.
You would have to be autistic to understand.

What is it like to see the world
Through different eyes than everyone else?
Where enjoyment is in the simplest of things,
Where stress and deadlines are not heard of or understood.
Where smells, sights, and sounds are what make up
The essence, and within these a world of enjoyment is yours.
Laughter and smiles rule your world.
You would have to be autistic to understand.

9/17/2002

Lisa A. Edelbrock

Mourning

It is very quiet;
You yearn to believe.
So when they are small
You believe he will catch up, he is okay.

As the years go by,
He misses the milestones.
Although you don't tell others,
They are noted in your mind.
The things he cannot do yet.
You mourn the loss.

Then one day at ten years old
It startles you awake,
And hits you in your heart.
While watching others at a park,
A parade, a picnic, at a pool.

He is not like the others,
He hasn't caught up.
He doesn't run or play like the other children,
Doesn't share his day, go out to play,
Have overnights with friends.
He is alone.
It all becomes so very clear:
No longer can denial hide the fact,
That this child is disabled,
And again you mourn the loss.

When the normal becomes the abnormal,
When you realize he does well for him,
But look where he should be.

You know you shouldn't think this way,
Shouldn't compare him to his peers.
It is not like you hadn't noticed.
But one day when you hug him,
You realize
He is not a small boy any longer.

The hopes of catching up are gone,
Replaced by the heartbreaking reality
That your child will never be like the others,
And again you mourn the loss.

Then tomorrow the abnormal turns
To the normal once again.

But in days and years to follow,
Again you will mourn the loss.

8/6/2001

Lisa A. Edelbrock

Unspoken Love

Everyday is such a struggle
In this silent world in which you live,
Where changes in routine
Will sometimes be your doom.

Yet you struggle with your signing,
And your seizures take their toll.
But your spirit glimmers through
In this smiling green-eyed boy.

Those smiles, laughs, and hugs,
And the twinkle in your eyes;
You find your ways of showing
The love you have inside.

You've taken us on this path
We didn't expect to travel.
I love you for your strength
And determination through it all.

What a gentle, loving soul!
I'm so very proud of you!!
I love you more than words;
To watch you, how it hurts.
This gentle, loving soul
In his quiet, difficult world.

I just wanted you to know:
I will always stand beside you.
Be your voice when one is needed.
Hold you in time of need,
And love you every minute
On this journey that you lead.

I LOVE YOU, SHELBY!
LOVE MOM
2/1998

Sweet Dreams

When I tucked you in tonight
There was sadness in your eyes.
Your gaze caught mine,
And there I saw sadness,
Your eyes they filled with tears;
Your chin began to quiver so,
And the tears did flow.

I wish that you could tell me
What makes you oh so sad?
I wish that you could share with me
The experiences of your day.
I wish you could tell me
What kids teased you at school today,
Or what child helped you,
Took you under their wing.
I wish you could share what your day was like–
Your friends, your dreams, and all those
Other boyish things.

Instead I hold you tight,
And wipe away your tears.
I hold you tight and tell you everything
Will be all right.

I let you know I love you;
I hope that is enough.
I hold you for a short time
And off to sleep you slip.
When I leave this sleeping soul
There is a smile spread across your cheeks.
To you, my love, be strong;
For this day at least
Our love did conquer all.

5/21/2002

Lisa A. Edelbrock

Changing Seasons

With the changing of the seasons
I now see changes in you.
The green has turned to a radiant splendor
And you, my son, turning more
Radiant each passing day.
Growing taller and smarter,
And unsteadied, too.

As the fall turns to winter I see
Your steadiness turn to uncertainty.
The storm clouds of winter
Have matched the storms that rage inside of you.
You no longer can express your wants and needs,
And your unsteadiness rises high.
I know not where this season takes us,
Nor do I know the reasons why.
All I can do is watch in earnest
And try to figure you out.
And hopefully with the
Return of spring
Your moods will swing
To where we can read them again.
And with the spring we can find
Some hope that you will be
Bright and beautiful,
Just as the tulips return in the spring.
We wait with earnest for
Your personality to become steady again.

9/2002

Storm Cloud on the Horizon

I'm not sure how to handle
These interruptions every day.
How many days can one leave work
And still be employed the next day?
I'm not sure how to handle these
Fits of anger and scenes of rage.
I'm not sure how to help you
Through your frustration and your pain.
I know you surely don't understand
All the chaos that you cause.
I know you don't understand
The concern within my eyes.
If you continue to act out, my child,
I don't know what to do next.
I don't want to send you to a home,
Because ours would be empty then.
I would miss you in my life
All too terribly.
I just wish that you could help me
Find this next leg of our journey.
But then again, maybe this next
Portion of the journey
Has already just begun.
Maybe you are already being
Instrumental in the life that is planned for us.
Maybe I just need to take
A few steps back and wait.
Life is less chaotic,
I can get a better look.
When I am not in the eye of the storm,
When I can see the whole picture.
Maybe after all these years
The needs of the many now outweigh
The needs of the one.

10/2002

Lisa A. Edelbrock

Life Being Simple

The smell of a child,
The touch of a child,
As they reach for your hand.
The gesture of pure confidence
And love.
The purity of a child's smile
And beauty of their laughter.
They ignite your feelings of life,
Love, and the very simple pleasures.

Life is not simple in this
Difficult, quiet world.
Struggles are difficult, behaviors
Hard to handle.
Even wrong and right,
Nothing is simple anymore.

I still crave his laughter, his smiles,
His smells.
I reach to hold his hand
It comforts me now,
More than for him.
Because nothing is simple
Anymore,
Except for this child's grin.

8/28/2002

Hopes and Dreams

"What are your hopes and dreams
For your child?"
The school note just quickly asked.

A simple question really,
But you didn't leave enough room.
My tears already forming
As I ponder the next move.

How does one explain? I want
What every parent wants:
A child who is liked,
Does well in school.
Makes every parent proud.
That is really what I want.
How can I explain I haven't given
Up that dream?
But how do I put into words
This day's reality?

I want to hear him talk.
I want to see him having friends.
I want him to play ball–
(I'm not particular on which kind.)
I want to watch him add, subtract,
And even multiply.
I want to see him excel in school,
Have some buddies who will kick around.
I would like to hear him say,
"I really love you Mom!"
I would like to see him date
And marry when he's grown.
But these are silly dreams–
Did you really want to know?

Lisa A. Edelbrock

How do I replace these dreams?
I just can't seem to let them go.

I just really don't want him
To always be alone.

9/2002

54   Lisa A. Edelbrock

PASSAGE THREE

My Gift

"And all that God created
was good."
~*Genesis,* Chapter One~

My Golden Ray

It was the summer of 1998, on the day Shelby was to turn eight.
We were scheduled for another sleep-deprived EEG.
We managed to keep him up all night
With many diversions and much foresight.
We made the long trip to the hospital with
A few stops to keep him awake.
We have learned from our previous visits
That if Shelby did not fall asleep when he was told
That we would have to reschedule
And then sedate him to get this test completed.

We entered the room with this tired little boy
And put him on the gurney to get all hooked up for the EEG.
This was no small feat to hold him down while they wired his head
In order to get the readings they needed.

Now he was given the okay to finally find his sleep.
As I lay beside him trying to comfort and relax this wired yet tired child,
I prayed to God to please help us,
To allow Shelby to relax so he could fall asleep.
I didn't think we could redo all this work that had gotten us to this point.
Life was becoming way too difficult.
I prayed for strength and help in his small, dimly-lit room.
As Shelby struggled to relax, to me appeared a golden ray
That slowly made its way to this struggling little child.
At the moment the ray touched his face he instantly drifted off to sleep.
At that moment a calm came over him and me, and I knew
We would be okay.
There he appeared to me, this little lightened face,
A face so perfect sleeping.
I saw the purity in his face and
I loved him even more.

Lisa A. Edelbrock

I am now more sure of this role than anything else in my life.
I understand my gift. The privilege has been explained to me.
A deeper love for this child evolved in that dimly-lit room that day.
Sometimes these miracles hide from those who cannot see.
I am helping God, you see, with this precious soul, which was given to me.
A great gift was given to me that day.
I see this child in a different light.
It doesn't mean I don't have bad days.
Days I wonder, and I grieve.
But I always see the gift now, my son, the golden ray.

Reflection

Sometimes it is hard to see,
What is directly in front of thee.

The forest through the trees.
The child through the disability.

Sometimes we need a little help.
And that is where

Hope enters
And Love lets us see

The gift in front of me!

May 2002

Lisa A. Edelbrock

The Messenger

Destiny

A date is made for us two to meet.
I wait with anticipation.
I wonder what he'll look like,
If he'll be funny and kind.

We meet that determined day,
And upon sight I fall in love!

Since that day we have been inseparable.
We laugh and love being together.

You've taken me where
I never thought I would go.
We have been through much,
The good and the bad.

We have made trips and adventured far.
Our journey together continues.
You have made me strong,
And helped me to learn of myself.

You are the love of my life!
You are my spirit,
You are my son.

We start our adventure
Knowing little of one another.
We learn of each other and
Know each other and what
Makes the other happy.

We travel through many mountains,
Up many rocky hills.
We see the beauty of every day unfold.

Lisa A. Edelbrock

We rejoice in the small accomplishments
And cherish every moment together.
I know this journey will not continue much longer.
Enjoy the company;
The spirit of the traveler
Capture the smiles in your heart.
Memorize the sounds and sights.
Although we continue on our journey,
It is not with as much difficulty as before.

The wear and tear has taken its toll on both of us.
Yet we are determined.
We continue on our quest.

Our quest is somewhat different than others.
We will climb no real mountains,
Play no little league, no football games,
No sleepovers, no first dates.

Our quest, however simple:
To hear the words:
"I love you."
To help this young man to be
The best he can be.
To have his voice be heard.

We are on the journey of life.
We will continue together forever.
You will always remain in my heart.
We will always have a very special bond.

2001

Different Worlds

To those who look from the outside,
What a strange world we must live in.
They wonder how we do it,
Say they could never do
What we do here everyday.

Our lives are not like theirs;
No resemblance can be seen.
We make compromises every day;
Our households do not run the same.
There are pictures plastered on the walls,
Signs posted here and there.
Schedules to be kept,
To keep his world more quiet,
Quiet, but complex.

Keep one step ahead;
Try to figure it all out.
Try to know what he'll react to;
What will cause him to act out?
What will calm this restless child
In his world filled with fears?
Just try to keep two steps ahead.
Try to keep an even keel.

There are those times
When no matter how well we plan,
Our world, it falls apart.
Our world becomes entangled,
His emotions run the gamut
Of smiles, tears and fears.

Lisa A. Edelbrock

All we can do is
Wait them out.
Try to calm and comfort
And watch the turmoil rage in
The eyes of the child
Lost in his small world.

Yes, our world is not the same,
Difficult– this is true.
Yet still our spirits soar,
For love will see us through.

Lisa A. Edelbrock

Just Simply Be

I remember when one was four months old, the other two years old.
She held his hand by the Christmas tree,
So proud just simply to be.

Through the years of laughing, growing, playing,
She now stands over five feet tall
And he maybe a foot shorter.
A teenager now, and a young man.
The years have changed them~
When they grew I do not know.
The years did seem to fly.

As I watch them play these days
There are hints of yesteryear.
There is also a grace in that young face.
Knowledge very few have,
A gentleness, a wiseness, patience far beyond her years.

This journey has changed us all.
I wonder what she would be like, sometimes,
If this world of ours were different.
She is all I ever dreamed of.
All I could have hoped for.
She has gained so much, loved so much,
Learned so much.

She realizes now that as she grows
And learns new things, that he is left behind.
She knows of the difficulties, knows of the trials.
As the years break the distance between these two souls,
One thing I know is true.

She is happier now and will always be
As proud to stand next to her brother
And just simply be.

5/20/2002

Faith

This charge so meek and mild.

Oh, my God,
What a wonderful child.
To trust me so completely,
To love
Unconditionally.

What a faithful follower to me.

Oh, my God,
How you must lead me.

The responsibility of this child
At times so overwhelming.
But his faith and trust in me now
Leads me on.

For I cannot do this alone.
Your strength will lead me on.
The path will be lightened,
For You know I need you too.

Once a follower,
Now a leader,
I put my faith in You.

Lead us on...

Lisa A. Edelbrock

Noble Friend

How do you tell someone how eternally indebted you are?
How do you explain that without them you would be lost?

That they are your light,
They are part of your soul,
They make up the true you?

That without them you would not be the same?
That without the heartache you would not be in
The same place, not have the same empathy?

Your spirit would not sing the same song;
Your dance would not be as alive.
True, the roads would be different,
But then I, and we, would not be.

You, my son, are my light;
You are my noble friend.

If only I could tell you, and then you'd understand;
But then again you probably already do.

For you see in my soul what I cannot see
And gently, very firmly, you
Pull it out and make me see for myself.

You, my son, are my noble friend,
And others say you don't understand.
You have been blessed with what we
Cannot see. You have been blessed
With divinity.

You are my individual, indisputable, connection
To the Divine.
We are shaped and molded,
By whom and what we love.

8/2002

Lisa A. Edelbrock

Simple Pleasures

I think that they are wrong.
I think that when they stare at us
They just don't seem to see.
We have a simple, complex life,
Something they just can't comprehend.

You dance at any music
And don't care who is standing there,
Or where you are at that
Very moment,
When the music finds you there.

You don't care what others think
When you laugh at silly things.

You find love and happiness
In the very simple things.
You watch as the bubbles catch
The wind and gently fly away.
You watch the bubbles rise
And catch the sun's rays.

We lay on the grass and watch
The light filter through the trees.
You find great comfort in the smell
Of someone else's hair.

You are not afraid to ask for a big hug.
When you're alone or when you seem a little scared.

You don't care what brand of clothes
You wear or the newest stylish hair.
You are individually you,
And don't bother what others think.

Maybe if we all
Just slowed down and took a look.
Maybe if we just let ourselves be kids
We'd all have happiness to spare.

You have found the deepest meaning
In this life we are here to live.
"Be true to self" is utmost,
And that is exactly what you give.

You give of yourself everyday.
You hide not a speck of yourself.
Why change this perfect child?
Let his spirit shine on through!
I love your laugh, your smile,
You are something special this is true!
Not as others think you are special,

The special love, child,
Is you!

10/2002

Lisa A. Edelbrock

Birthday

God has changed the grief, you see,
Into the gift I did not see.
Oh, the view so wonderfully!!

The grief is gone,
The child seen.
A gift from God,
Reborn, you see.
Not in life,
But in my eyes.

My soul he touched today
And on this, his birthday.

The grief is gone;
Time to celebrate
The child who's here
Standing by my side.
The smiling lad, with big green eyes.

For now I clearly see
The task in front of me.
To lead this child, so meek and mild,
Carefully to the other side.

If he only really knew
Who indeed
Is leading whom!

Lisa A. Edelbrock

PASSAGE FOUR

Listening

God's one
and only
voice is
Silence

Lisa A. Edelbrock

The Witness

Does Shelby speak to God?
Do they have a bond?
Shelby loves to go to church,
Does he heed God's call?

Does the kingdom of heaven
Belong to these different children
That God has quietly sent?
Does God send these angels
To us from far above
To be His witness
Of Faith, of Hope, and Love?

Do we care for and accept these children
Or turn the other cheek?
Do you listen to their message,
Or do you stare and sneer and tease?
Do you see what has been given?
Do you slowly look around?

Have you been blessed with healthy children
Who laugh and play and run?

Have you been richly blessed
By his presence with you today?
Is your blessing a small angel,
Disguised as a small child?

Do you sometimes feel a spirit?
Do you sometimes see his light?
Do you sometimes even wonder
What his life is all about?

He stands there right before you.
Just take a deeper look.
If you were God just who would you really send,
To be a true witness
Of Faith, of Hope, of Love?

Just take a deeper look.
For you are richly blessed.

June 2002

Lisa A. Edelbrock

My Purpose

You are my purpose in this life.
The mystery, and the mystical.
The purpose and the reason.

Every day is an adventure,
Every day you teach me
New things about you, about me;
About our world.

You are extraordinary!
You amaze me;
You fill me with wonder.
You and your world captivate me.

I want to know more.
I want to know you better.
I love your essence;
I love you.

5/2002

Lisa A. Edelbrock

Roads Less Traveled

The days are filled with trials,
Of trying to keep up.
Trying to figure the next step,
We of the road less traveled.
The road is less paved than others,
The road less understood.
The road, but oh so remarkable,
For those traveling straight uphill.
The hardships, there are many,
And often misunderstood.
Take time to see the silver
On the lining of the clouds.
I wouldn't change direction,
Even if it were allowed.
The gifts they are so plentiful,
All we need to do is look.
In the eyes of the traveler we are guiding
To find his little nook.

The traveler, he is special;
In the silent world he lives.
But oh, for such a small one,
The spirit that he gives!
For deep inside he holds the meaning
Of this difficult life he lives.
For true love will release us
As we travel straight and tall.

7/2000

Heaven's Gift

Last week I had such grief
Over the words he'll never speak.

But now I see the lighted face
Of this small child with gifted grace.
You've revealed Yourself to me–
Oh, how precious he must be.

For in that moment now I see the
Task you have in front of me.
Oh, the faith you have put in me,
To guide this child
Endlessly.

But when I stopped and looked.
The beauty there–
God, my soul it shook.

For now I understand
The gift that I've been given.

The privilege mine…

Your gift from heaven.

1999

Lisa A. Edelbrock

Footsteps

The footsteps patter~
The nine-year-old is up.
As I gently nudge him back to bed,
A bathroom break.

As he sits and looks at me, with big green eyes and
The childish grin, the giggles begin.
The best laugh I have heard in years.
He signs for pop and I nestle him back into bed.
Again he looks and the giggles begin.

What's in that mind that makes you laugh?
Please share with me the joke.
The giggles they continue from deep within your soul.
The twinkle and more giggles, trying so hard not to choke.

The giggles and those big green eyes,
What a wary sight you are.
I finally tuck you back in bed, and now again you dream~
But here I sit and wonder at 1 a.m.
Just what made you grin?

I wish you could share with me,
But for now,
I love you, and that giggle.

One Voice

How many times have we thought,
"If only I could have some quiet time,
Some peace?"

But then there are those who have
Prayed for noise,
One voice.
What can one voice do?
Fill a mother's heart with joy,
Fulfill a dream,
Open a world.

Some will never understand the pain and sorrow,
The wondering just what this child
Would really sound like.
Some will never understand the loss.
Some will never understand this gift,
How it has changed every aspect of our lives,
Has changed us all for the better.

Some will never understand
How one still yearns, still hopes, still dreams.

Some will understand
The love.

2001

Lisa A. Edelbrock

Imprint

One day this boy arrives,
Your assignment for the year.
You have to understand the leading
Role you are set to play.

These children look for guidance
In this difficult world they live in.
They look for hope and love
In their world of struggles.

You come with many labels:
Aides, teachers, helpers, paraprofessionals.

Your job is all the same,
To guide this youngster on,
To be his helper and his friend.

They lead a difficult life,
These hardened little souls.
No voice, no sound, no vision,
Difficult in writing, reading, even sitting.
In this place of life called school.

These helpers have much patience.
You learn the tasks and more.
You guide, you teach, you learn
How to adapt for little hands.

Then one day your job is over.
This child leaves your world–
A little bigger, a little stronger,
In their quiet difficult world.

For the families that you help
There are no words to say:"thank-you"
For your love, your fears, your tears,
Your worries– for speaking up to help.
For guiding this little soul,
In this difficult world that is his.

When you stop and ponder about
The marvel of this child,
You really need to wonder
"Just who really did teach whom?"

One thing you must understand
Although this child moves on,
Your heart is touched forever,
And his imprint lingers on.

6/2000

Lisa A. Edelbrock

An Amazing Child

What a wonder you are!
I watch you these days,
Trying to figure it all out.

Then you do something
That totally blows me away.
You make a sign, you verbalize,
You let me know you're still trying.
You have thoughts, hopes and dreams,
And you
Are this amazing child.

Amazing for all that is expected,
All that is asked.
What a wonderful personality,
What a caring soul.
So obscure, yet all so there.

I watch at times to see
You think and dream~
Just what makes you click?
And then you smile,
And again I'm left to ponder
With total amazement

How truly special you are.

Lisa A. Edelbrock

A Thousand Words

"A picture speaks a thousand words,"
Or so the saying goes.

So this flickering green-eyed boy
Tells a thousand fold.
His eyes they hold the mystery
Of the thoughts we'll never know,
Of things he holds so deeply,
The tears for which we ponder
As they trickle down his smooth, soft skin.

At times I watch intently, and take in his smell and being.
There is much that makes up this quiet little man.

If pictures speak a thousand words,
I need to know the rest.
Speak to me now, Shelby;
Tell me of your world.

Tell me why you giggle;
Tell my why you cry;
Speak to me of dreams,
Of wants and how's and why's.
Tell me of your spirit;
I want to know it all.
Tell me of your soul
That is hidden deep inside.

I know so very little, and that I have had to guess.
We've been through much together;
I know so very little of really what makes you tick.

I want to know with whom I journey.

If pictures speak a thousand words,
I'll take another roll.

Love's Voice

Every evening the same pattern:
Shower, then to bed.
I lay with you gently,
Read a book,
Then off to sleep you go.

I say, "I love you, Shelby."
He gently nods a yes.

The shower, then to bed.
I lay with you gently,
Read a book,
Then off to sleep you start to go.
I bend over this drifting child;
He reaches for the cross
Permanently worn around my neck,
Pulls me slightly to him,
"Auho ove ooh—"
Not understanding
I say, "What sweetie?"
"Ar ove ooh"

For the first time in eleven years
He has initiated, and spoken
The words I have
Waited a lifetime to hear.
"I love you too, Shelby!"
As he smiles and closes his sleepy eyes,
And drifts off to the dreams
That await him.

Lisa A. Edelbrock

What a wonder this child is.
I wish I could capture that moment
And replay it over and over again.
Will I hear those words

Initiated by him again?
Or is this the one and only?

Capture that moment,
Hold it close,
For then I can replay it in my mind and heart
For many years to come.

6/12/2002

For This I Truly Know

In your presence
Is where I am truly meant to be.
My heart, it slows.
My breath is deep.
I cherish the glimmering of your face.
These moments will never happen again.

This life we live
Is all we have:
We are meant to be.

I questioned destiny many times,
But deep inside I knew.

You were meant for me, my son,
And I am blessed by you!

Lisa A. Edelbrock

Warriors of Hope

Am I the only one who sees them?
Look into their eyes,
The window to the soul.

The toughness, the sadness, the loss,
The hope.
The never-ending love.

The walking wounded,
The warriors of hope.

The sadness that breaks through,
In the quiet lonely times.
The wish for miracles,
And for past "If only's."

Tired, sad, lost,
Desperate at times.

These warriors of hope.

They continue to fight
Even in the hardest and lowest
Of times.
They fight with the very breath
They breathe.
For they fight for the life
They cherish above their own—
Mothers, fathers, brothers, sisters,
Grandfathers, and grandmothers.

These are the warriors of hope.

5/11/2002

Lisa A. Edelbrock

PASSAGE FIVE

Heartstrings

The ties
that bind
our hearts

The Future

She cries at night like I do,
For what the future holds,
Unsure of all we will
Someday enter into.
Then one night all unexpectedly,
She calls for me before she drifts off to sleep:
"When Dad dies, Mom, Shelby will be sad;
When you die, Mom, Shelby will
be even sadder.
When I die, Mom, Shelby will be lost."
We both cry tears at the thought of Shelby all alone.

Then I try to comfort and explain, we know
Not what the future brings.
We should try not to worry, because we have
No control over those things.
I try to comfort with the thought
That we do not know the order.
Maybe Shelby will die first, and
Then we will no longer need to worry about him.
It is sad to think this is a comforting thought
To each of us this evening.
But it is the truth, and it is what comforts us.
Our angel would be with God,
And we would have no cause to worry.

I go to bed this evening,
Thinking of my daughter.
What difficult thoughts for a young girl to have,
What difficult worries for a child so young.
She is wise beyond her years.
However, I also see her age before she should.

Lisa A. Edelbrock

I have not told her yet–
I pray that she will look after her brother
When her father and I have gone.
I pray she will be there for him,
Help him through the difficult times.
Visit him and make sure he has all he should.
I pray she will take on this huge responsibility.
It is difficult to ask this of her;
I also know she will be up for the task.
She has a heart of gold,
And her mere presence makes me smile.
She will be there for him;
I know this is true.
She will love him
As much,
If not more,
In a different way, but still
Love him more
Than I ever could.

9/2002

This I Know

All I know is I love the feel of you.
I love the way you make me feel,
And the way I touch you so.

You came into my life,
And I haven't been able
To shake the feel of you.
I try to live without you,
But your spirit haunts me so.
I try to get along with life,
But your memory
Brings me back to you.
I yearn for your presence,
Your spirit, your essence.
I love the thought of you.

I wish we could change our
Lots in life.
But that is not how this
Life works.

All I know~
Is I love the feel of you.
All I know~
Is I love the smell of you.
All I know~
Is your spirit lightens my soul.
All I know~
Is what true love is.
And what we had was real.
This I know~
I will always love you so.

Lisa A. Edelbrock

No matter where your spirit goes;
No matter where you live.
This I know~
My heart is still tied to you.
I wish I could explain
To you what my life is like
Without you very near.

All I can really do
Is write and let my love flow out
To the pen and paper now,
Hoping someday you will read these
Words and know
They were meant for you.

This I know~
I will always love you so!

11/23/2002

HAPPY MOTHER'S DAY

Dear Mom,

Sometimes you may get discouraged

Because I am so small,

And always leave my fingerprints

On furniture, windows, and walls.

But everyday I'm growing up

And soon I'll be so tall,

That all those little handprints

Will be hard to recall.

So here's a special handprint

Just so that you can say,

This is how my fingers looked

When I placed them here today!

Love, Shelby
May 8, 1991

98

Lisa A. Edelbrock

Mother's Day

I remember each day vividly.
The excitement when my first child,
My daughter, was born.
The sheer happiness when she cried and
Entered this world.

I remember also the total exhaustion
When my son was born.
So drained, but when he finally
Took that breath.
How relieved and thrilled I was.

That was many years ago, but the
Memories bring me back to yesterday.
I remember my mother saying,
"Oh, the woes of motherhood."
I thought then, how melodramatic it was
Of her– too many kids.
"It can't be all that bad."

Now I realize what she was trying to tell me.
She was trying to ready me for the sorrow.

The early years of nighttime feedings.
Sick children, little sleep, and household chores.
She could never in a million years prepare me
For my son.

The day they diagnosed him, my heart shattered–
Too many pieces to put together again.
The tears flow freely now,
Each month a new goal, hoping to master a few
Old goals, before new ones are added.
Each week brings a new disaster,
Each day a new struggle.

The goals met easily by one child
Remain unfulfilled by the other.
As his sister tells of school and friends,
He sits quietly with no words,
No friends to speak of.

Each day so much a struggle to keep him on course.
Still learning–pushing to be the most he can be
With the limits that have seemingly been placed.

There are the giggles and smiles of childhood,
The joys of bonfires at night, a good Disney movie,
And snuggling before he drifts off to sleep.

These are the joys and woes of motherhood.
If I had a chance to do it all again,
Would I?
Could I?

–In a minute!
For these are my children,
My joys and my sorrows.

These do not diminish the love when I look into
Their childhood faces,
Those faces where there are traces of me.
I created these two precious souls.
They are a part of me.

They will always be a part of me.
And that is the joy that I give to
Myself today.
These two souls are mine
On Mother's Day!

5/11/2002

Lisa A. Edelbrock

Guardian

You were the first to touch this child.
You were the first to heal.
You were the first to explain
To us parents
This child lives in a different world.

You are the understanding doctor.
You are the one who sees.
You are the one who asks the questions.
You are the one who heals.

You have traced this child's path,
His progression through the years.
You are still the one, who asks,
And more importantly understands.
You know what we will run into;
You know the problems we'll have.
You know the questions I have
And the fears that I hide from
The rest of the world,
For I know they can't even begin to understand.

You are the doctor who changed his schedule,
The one to make us the exception.
You gave and hoped with us.
I could see it in your face
And felt your compassion linger
As we sat and chatted,
As you took his blood more than once.
To you it seemed a small thing;
To us it made this one thing easier
When the rest of our world was falling apart.

Lisa A. Edelbrock

You were the reassurance needed
Among all the other white coats.
Not all of them were good;
Not all were compassionate.
Some misunderstood;
Some hid us from the details;
Some hid us from the truth.

But you were our guardian savior,
Amongst all the tests and trials.
Amongst all the technical jargon.
You were the one we asked for;
You were our shining light.
You were the one we brought
M&M's to,
Because you are the one
Who made a difference;
You are the one that cared!

10/5/2002

Lisa A. Edelbrock

Heartbreak

What would I be
Without the souls I see?
These two gifts I did receive.

I love them so,
So much as to ever truly understand.

The loss some parents must feel
When they lose a child.

Or the hurt when one knows
They must leave these souls behind.
They must go on without them.
The heartbreak it must be.

When you know you'll not be there
To see them grow,
Please take them with you in your heart
So this parent won't be left alone.

Lisa A. Edelbrock

Family's Loss

We smiled, laughed and played.
Now all of a sudden you are gone.
We all know of that empty nest syndrome,
But no, it's not the same.
When that little one is special
There is just no easy way.

All my energy was focused
On this small lad that I led.
My days and nights engulfed
By the mission that lay ahead,

To see you safely through
Your life that lay ahead.
Now your bed lies empty.
My soul for you it weeps;
My love for you still endless.

I yearn to hear your voice,
To touch and smell your hair,
To look into your eyes,
To feel your presence here.

Where do I place this loss
That engulfs me every day?
My energy once all charged,
Now lingers as I pray.

My job now with you is done.
My angel has flown home.

I did the very best I could, God.
In Faith, in Hope, in Love.

5/2002

If You Were The One

They are our family; this is true,
But what do they really know
Of our life's trials and how autism
Has pierced our inner soul?

They know not of the tears we've shed
Or the trials along the way.
They know not of the fears we bear
Or the future that lays ahead.
They know not of the hardships,
Our daily lives we live.
They know little of our lives
We do not keep it secretly.
They know not of the meetings
We have nearly every week,
Just trying to get through school
And the problems that are perceived.

They know not of our battle
With tears and fears and thoughts:
"What will his life be like
When he is an adult?"
No, he will not live like his cousins
Who run and play.
No, he'll never marry or move very far away.

They are family, this is true,
But really what do they know?

When talk is made at gatherings,
Really what can one say?
Do they really want to know?
My child is bound to be alone,
All his natural days.

Lisa A. Edelbrock

Our lives are not like yours,
Do you dare to take an inner look?
Do our lives somehow scare you?
For you know this could be you.
Do the complications stir you
To take a deeper look
At what your values are?
Your inner soul lies there.

If you had to be the one,
Could your love be standing still?
Could your family remain intact?
Could you deal with all who stare?
Could you change your life
To revolve around just this one endangered soul?
Could you enrich his spirit?
And heal yours while you're there?
Could you deal with what needs to be done?
And not ponder on do you dare?
Could you deal with this life we live
If really you were the one?

Could your life be changed in a moment,
When things get out of hand?
Could you remain cool and calm,
And always two steps ahead?

Would your inner strength be challenged?
Could it remain as strong?
Or would it be even stronger, stronger because you are the one.

Could you dare to believe all God makes is good,
Dare to believe this is God's plan?
No control over the destiny that was planned out years ahead.
Could you dare to believe God makes no mistakes?
This is His almighty plan.

The Messenger

Could you have the stamina or
The vigilance that it takes?
Do you have the strength to walk unwavering
As you lead this little stray?

Take a look inside yourself
And ponder all I've asked.
Would you? Could you?
If really you were the one?

Could you look at this young lad
And see a spirit there?
Could you see God's gift
Standing next to you, holding your hand?
Could you live our life?
Feel His presence here?
Look into your heart
And see what truth lies there;
Could you live our life
If really you were the one?

8/30/2002

Lisa A. Edelbrock

The Messenger

Ella, A Grand Lady

I don't think she knew
How I looked to her for strength.
I don't think she knew
How I looked to her for courage.
I don't think she knew
That her presence gave me solace
And an inner peace.

She was old, and worn.
Her voice gone long ago,
Her eyes now failing,
And looking very weary now.
We talked at times of loneliness,
And years that went before.
But it was that last brief visit
That I remember so.

I walked into her hospital room,
And there she gently slept.
She slept there, oh, so slightly–
Her humanity and age
Now came shining through.
"I will wake her", a nurse whispered quietly.
"She can sleep after you have left."

We spoke then of her tiredness,
And her wish to go to heaven soon.
We spoke then of her strength
And all that she'd been through.
And then she surprised me when she said,

Lisa A. Edelbrock

"You have a great strength my child.
I couldn't do what you have done;
You have great love, my child.
I'm so very proud of you."
I sat there then in awe at the words that she had said.
"You have a determination and strength
That far outstretches mine."
The woman I had looked to for strength
Was now applauding mine.
In that quiet moment, I felt she understood
What had been given, what had been taken,
And all that we had been through.

We sat quietly and gently held each other's hands.
The worn and wrinkled hands that had seen
Many years and endured some awful things.
When she touched my hands,
I knew she was giving me her strength,
And then she quietly said, I need to rest some more now.
And then we said good-bye
And kissed each other's cheek,
As grandmas always do.

There must have been a reason why I went
And visited her that day.
I will always remember that visit
And the strength to me she gave.
I think of her quite often.
I think she would still be proud.

I miss you still, Grandma,
I'm an Edelbrock,
And I will make you proud.

8/30/2002

To My Mother This Mother's Day

I now know what you were trying to say:
Hold on to your heart my child!
For your child will break it and take it someday.
Be strong, be true, and never tire;
There is much to do in being a mother.
There will be smiles of joy
And tears of sorrow.
Your world, my dear, will never be the same.
You will need to give and give, and give some more.
There is much effort in being a very good mom.

You forgot to mention a few things, though, Mom.
You forgot the overwhelming feeling of a true big hug.
The warm smiles, the laughter your own child brings.
Knowing only Mom can make things better.
The pride in seeing them accomplish that overwhelming task.
And most of all hearing comfort and truth in
"I love you Mom" in your child's voice.
But you were right, Mom.
I lost my heart that very first day.
There have been smiles of laughter and
Tears of sorrow.

My simple gift to you today
With more comfort now than years before,
In acknowledgement of all you have been,
And all you have done.
Knowing now it was no easy task.

Happy Mother's Day,
With heartfelt pride,
That you are my Mom.

5/11/2002

Lisa A. Edelbrock

Calming Spirit

This quiet reassuring man,
Gentleness in his hand.

A harbor when the winds start to blow.
A beacon, calling us towards home.

This man who's filled with gentle grace,
Whose mere presence fills us with peace.

Known as Grandpa to these kindred spirits
Who yearn for his presence
And his peaceful spirit.

Always there to lend a hand,
To reassure a wondering soul.

Thank you, Dad, for being there
With wisdom and grace
And heart wide open.

Lisa A. Edelbrock

Precious Gifts

To reach for the stars,
To believe in myself.

That life is not always happy,
And not always fair.
That motherhood is smiles and tears.

That with prayer there is hope,
With hope there is peace,
With peace there is calm,
With calm is reflection.

With reflection is the understanding.
That within me is courage,
Within me is strength.

The strength to persevere
For what I believe is right
And to fight for those I love.

That family remains a loyal constant,
That love is the master key.

And as always~
Mom is always there
And my loyal friend.

Your love will live on by the values
That have been embedded.

I can only hope to give my children
All the wonderful gifts you have
Given me,

Your grateful and
Admiring daughter.

5/2001

Greetings

When people ask, "Just how is Shelby doing?"
How much do they want to know?
If I say he's doing fine,
He is very good.
Do they then think that he can talk?
So I need to answer carefully,
So they don't think that he is cured,
So they know that he is holding his own,
But that his life is not like theirs.
Do they really want to know
All the day-to-day struggles we have?
Or are they just being polite in asking
"How is Shelby doing?"
It's hard to read their faces, and some I
Really can't tell.
They really couldn't deal with the news
If I gave them all the details.

So, "Shelby is doing good!
He just doesn't talk."
I leave them with that update,
For these acquaintances of mine,
The people who really want to know,
Really care how we are doing;
All they really need to do is watch,
Watch him in our world and how he deals
With the little things.
But most of all you can see it.
See it in our eyes, the window to the soul.
There is pain and sadness there, and the
Flittering thought of, you will never know.

Lisa A. Edelbrock

PASSAGE SIX

Thoughts Unspoken

Bearing
my
soul

Lisa A. Edelbrock

Symbolism

The symbolism is not lost on me.
I see the truth lying there.

He was chosen to be baby Jesus
When he was four months old.
I felt it such a privilege
For him to play this role.

Oh, how calm and quiet he was
As Mary held his hand.

Was he anointed from his birth?
Was this our little test?
Would we allow him to play
Someone who gave his life,
Someone who was misunderstood
But led others to believe?

I believe he was anointed, the day
That he was born.
He didn't breathe at first,
But then our prayers were answered
As he finally took that initial breath.

My ray of gold,
My ray of hope,
My individual, indisputable,
Connection to the Divine.
So many connections in his life,
Symbolism everywhere.

His message to deliver:
You are richly blessed
And not to give up hope.

2002

Perseverance

It was just a year ago
When we sat hooked to that hospital bed.
Able to be released on the day
That we all dread,
And is now locked in history
As September 11, 2001.

The year has been a good year;
No more meds for you to take.
Life has gotten simpler;
Maybe it is just all in my mind.

We still struggle with behaviors
And emotions that run wild.
But I can't help but see a child
Who really isn't wild.
Just a confused soul,
Trying to find his place
In this jumbled world
That doesn't stay the same.

The true fact of life is
That change is a certain constant.
But for you, my dear child,
That change creates such havoc.
I understand it is hard for you.
I try to ease you in;
Unfortunately, you must go
Some of these miles all alone.

Lisa A. Edelbrock

As you get bigger, it'll get harder
To protect you from this world,
People can be nice;
However, they can most certainly be harsh.

I try to give you all the tools
To help you understand,
To know you are a precious soul.
I know you will try hard;
You want so much to please.

You amaze me how
You never give up hope.
Your perseverance astonishes me
And gives my soul that jump start
To keep on hoping, dreaming.

Just seeing you,
This astonishing child,
Standing directly in front of me,
And never giving up,
Never letting life
Get the best of him,
Renews my hope in you
And gives great hope to me.

9/2002

Wind and Rain

I find myself longing for wind.

I am a mother,
A worker,
A thinker, a writer,
A creative soul
And a protector.

I dream of carefree days–
No therapies, no doctors;
I dream of warm sand shores,
Of the sun baking me with its warmth.
The sun melting my worries and
Dissipating my fears.

So I long for wind to take me to where
None of these problems exist,
Where there is only sunshine and the
Sense of freedom that comes
From a very long vacation.

But there are two small children sleeping,
Nestled safely in their beds.
Their dreams take them elsewhere.
I hear them mumble in their sleep.
I see them smile and hear their giggles
In the slumber they have reached.
They are safe and warm and they know
That I am always near.
They know I will not run,
Not ever disappear.
I am their constant.

Lisa A. Edelbrock

These two small souls are what keep me here.
They keep me grounded
In the midst of the battles that rage.
These two are what remind me of what really matters
In this world.

I fight these battles,
Engage,
For it is the dream of
Them flying free.
They anchor me here.

I still dream of wind to take
Me elsewhere,
To set me free.
And with the wind,
I hope for rain
To wash the pallet clean,
Just as the smell of
An early spring rain
Renews life and starts
Life over again.

I yearn for rain to do the same.
To cleanse my soul and set me free.
There are times I wish
That I could start over once again.

So I like the wind
And pray for rain
To help me start clean and fresh
And all renewed.

10/2002

The Messenger

Lisa A. Edelbrock

The Ride

We waited for what seemed like hours.
We walked the long aisle up.
Space Mountain we had reached.
You have to sit by yourself now.
Keep your hands inside.
I'll be right here, in back of you.
I hope he makes it through, I thought,
For there is no way to stop this ride.
The ride it was a fast one.
The turns, the flips, the curves.
All in the darkness, so we could
Never see what would happen next.
The lights they were magnificent, the
Thrills well worth the wait.
The turns were hard, we hit against the sides,
But you wanted more
When we reached that final halt.
I patted your shoulders in a
Reassuring gesture, "Are you okay?"
And "more" is all you signed,
More is all you asked.

Just like our life with you.
We waited a long time to enjoy this ride
We worked hard in getting to where we are.
So fast, so hard, so filled with splendor,
The bright lights,
The giggles and the laughs.
You keep us wanting more;
You keep us coming back.

10/9/2002

Life Is A Journey

Loss of childhood,
Loss of innocence,
Loss of adolescence,
Loss of mother and father,
Loss of the family unit,
Loss of a child,
Loss of how we thought our life would be,
Loss of dreams,
Loss of ourselves and the search to find
Who we really are.
It is how we deal with these losses that make
Us who we are.
Do we become bitter, cold, uncaring?
Or do we reach out?
Do we find comfort in those we love,
In those that care for us?

These trials of our soul mold us.
These trials are all difficult;
No one said it would be easy.

When we make it through the difficult times,
The happier times become so much sweeter.

Do we treat our loved ones respectfully, caring?
Do we treat them how we would like to be treated?
Do we like how we handled the last passage of our life?

It is not too late to change how we are reacting.
Life is a journey.

Lisa A. Edelbrock

We can always change the path we are on.
A small degree of change now will change our
Life by many degrees in years to come.
We will be changed by the changes we make in ourselves.

There is always someone who cares about you.
Love now, for love is never a mistake.

4/2002

Lisa A. Edelbrock

Meaning of Life

The meaning of life is very simple;
It is what makes your spirit sing.
That is what your destiny is,
So simple and so true.
Just listen with your heart,
Let your soul sing its song.
Do what you love to do.

Do what you need to free your soul,
Go where you need to go.

Do not let life pass, my friend,
With your song unsung,
Your spirit not free.
For this is truly your
Individual destiny.

So when your body returns to ashes,
Your song will still be sung,
And spirit flying free,
All on your wings of love.

8/25/2002

The Spirit

I prayed before for health and the perfection of this child.
Only thought to be let down by the mystery of the Lord.
But the cure that was prayed for was left to be unknown.

The blessing was bestowed
Long before we knew the path.
As to not reveal His secret,
He wrapped it in this child.

In asking for God's help,
The journey did begin.
Not of words to be told,
But of lessons that lie within.
He has taught us of ourselves
And what true love is all about.
Of seeing others deeply~
Not what they look like on the out.

But of the spirit that lies within
The beauty of this child,
To bring us close to God
In the treasure of a smile.

The paths have all been different,
The feelings all the same.
On the path each of you has taken
To find us here today.
Your ears did not hear his words,
But your hearts heard his call.

So listen with your heart,
And you will surely hear
The message from the boy
Who will never speak a word.

Lisa A. Edelbrock

Where words mean very little
And love the master key
To unlock this world he lives in
And to us a mystery.

He has touched you all in spirit
And called you each by name;
To share his wonderful journey,
Never again will you be the same.

Thank you all for being part of Shelby's
Travels through this life.
We appreciate your love and support.
May God bless you all!

Blossoming

In the early years there was such urgency
To get help fast,
Before it was too late,
Before we lost him forever.
A determination to get him to talk,
To be like all the others,
To live this "normal life."

In spite of all I've done,
Perhaps because of what I have done,
We have muddled through.
Children do grow,
Unfold, blossom.
They become who they were meant to be;
Their destiny is fulfilled.

I have spent years reaching forward,
Forward to my son,
Forward to find the truest him.
I have reached for him,
And he has reached for the world around him.
His life is not "normal" by any means.
But is one life superior to the other?

He is his truest self.
He has fought to become who he is.
He fights every day to remain who he is,
To keep his personality.
His life is built on simple things,
The love of his family,
Good Disney movies and just being free.

Lisa A. Edelbrock

I have reached him;
I have tried to give him the world.
He has taken the best parts of this world
And accepted them graciously.
Shelby has grown into his destiny,
And in turn he has set me free.
I know he will be okay,
He has this wonderful spirit
And is who he wants to be.

I have accepted the child and all that goes with him.
As Shelby continues his silence,
This does not mean we have not gained ground.
We have not failed.
He has found himself;
That is all we as parents can hope.
A delightful soul,
Passionate and tolerant,
He has found his place.
I am proud that he is who he is,
What he is,
Because it is the truest he can be.

We cannot change the daffodil
Into the purest rose.
We cannot change the red rose
Into a gracious yellow rose.
We can accept each flower,
And the beauty that each one brings
Into the flower garden,
And appreciate what each
Flower brings into the
Garden for it is being
The truest it can be.

10/9/2002

Lisa A. Edelbrock

Wings of Love

Put your focus on the path:
The journey is the reason
Why we are here for this lifetime;
It is the focus we must have.
Enjoy the journey;
Embrace the hardships and the trials.
We are here to learn of life,
Humanity and losses.
There is hope in the gesture given;
There is hope in a young man's smile.
There is hope in those who listened
And hope by those who have chosen
To give amounts of their time
To help an endangered child find his
Focus in this life.
There have been hundreds,
Perhaps thousands, who have helped
This angel find his wings.
Someday he will soar
The way that he was intended all along.
With such grace and beauty
And with the wings of love,
Embroidered from all those who
Helped this soul along
On this journey that he led to
Find the faith, the hope, and the love
That lifted him along the way.

10/9/2002

The Journey

I seek out stories and books of
Others along this journey.
It seems they all make extraordinary progress.
They are all complimented
On helping their children out of their silence.
And I along with many applaud
These grand endeavors.

What then are we to say to the parent
Who has done all these same programs,
Who has poured just as much of themselves
Into their lost child, and yet the silence remains?

I want to say to them now,
"We are not failures.
We have done all we could and more.
We continue every day to teach our children the
Language of the spirit and they continue
Every day to impress us with their patience,
With their determination, and they
Overwhelm us at times with their perseverance."

I want to say to the mothers and the fathers:
That the journey can be long.
However, there is still some passage
That the two of you must cross together.
That the journey will be completed some day,
So hold fast to your dreams.

I want to remind you there are others along
This journey that mourn with you,
Applaud with you,
Are overwhelmed with you,
And above all we continue to hope with you.

Lisa A. Edelbrock

Every parent of these unique and intriguing children
Will one day feel or hear the love this child has, that
You as their parents have nurtured and with gentle patience
Have helped your child to understand.

This book is dedicated to you,
The "warriors of hope."
You need to be applauded and told that yours is not
Any easy journey.
Yet you continue to hope
And to dream,
And have faith in this child,
When everyone else seems to lose theirs.

You and your children
Are the messengers of
Great faith,
Great hope,
And extraordinary love.

Enjoy your journey for it is this
Passage that you are destined to.
It is this experience that makes
Your life what it is.
Enjoy your messenger, for there will
Never be one as instrumental to you as him or her.

God Bless!

10/2002

Lisa A. Edelbrock

REFLECTIONS

"SEASONS OF CHANGE"

REFLECTIONS

"SEASONS OF CHANGE"